Every Dog's Dream Rescue

A portion of all profits earned from your purchase of this book will be sent to Every Dog's Dream Rescue, Inc., a group of compassionate volunteers working around the clock to provide a safe haven for all the animals that are bought into their rescue facility. Every Dog's Dream not only maintains high-quality care for rescued dogs; they also take in cats and small animals. They operate an adoption center located within the Petco facility on Harry L. Drive in Johnson City, New York, where they always have an abundance of cats and kittens and a number of puppies up for adoption. Every Dog's Dream helps families across New York State to care for stray cats. They also help provide food and veterinary care for those who cannot afford to pay but don't want to give up their animals.

To find out more or to donate, go to:
EveryDogsDream.org

Caring for Dogs

Village Earth Press

Copyright © 2017 by Village Earth Press, a division of Harding House Publishing.

All rights reserved. No part of this publication may be reproduced or transmitted in any form or by any means, electronic or mechanical, including photocopying, recording, taping, or any information storage and retrieval system, without permission from the publisher.

Village Earth Press
Vestal, New York 13850
www.villageearthpress.com

First Printing
9 8 7 6 5 4 3 2 1

ISBN: 978-1-62524-451-2
series ISBN: 978-1-62524-449-9

Author: Rae Simons
Design: Micaela Grace Sanna

Caring for Dogs

....
RAE SIMONS

TABLE OF CONTENTS:

Introduction	10
1. Dogs' Story	14
2. Finding Your New Best Friend	24
3. Keeping Your Dog Healthy	36
4. Understanding Your Dog	44

Introduction

To parents and teachers:

Animal lives matter. Human welfare and animal welfare are interwoven so tightly that they cannot be separated. In other words, what hurts animals will ultimately hurt us as well.

We can see this at the planetary level. As animals lose their habitats because of climate change, pollution, deforestation, and other factors, human well-being is also threatened. Sometimes, people seem to think it's an either-or situation: we either help people (by investing in businesses that are harming the environment) or we help animals (by hindering the success of those same businesses). That's not the way things work on our planet, though. We are all in this together. What puts animals at risk is an equal risk to human well-being.

We are not only linked to animals at the biological and environmental level. We also share many of the same emotions with them—and how we treat animals can't be separated from how we treat each other. Mark Bekoff, an evolutionary biologist, said in an interview with *Forbes* magazine:

> how we treat other animals has direct effects on how we feel about ourselves ...compassion begets compassion.... So, when we're nice to other animals and empathize compassionately with their physical and mental health we're also spreading compassion to other people.

The more scientists learn about animals, the more they find that the creatures with whom we share our planet are far more amazing than we ever knew. Scientists have proven that even fish are conscious and sentient; they've discovered that it's not only our dogs who are sensitive to our pain but that rats, mice, and even chickens are as well; and they also have proof that crows can use tools that are more sophisticated than chimpanzees'. What's more, based on animals' neurochemicals, our furred and feathered friends experience the same feelings of love that humans do.

Earlier cultures thought of animals as our brothers and sisters, but somehow, our culture lost track of that perspective. We need to regain it, not only for animals' sakes but for our own—and we need to teach it to our children. By teaching children how to care for animals (whether pets, farm animals, or wild animals), we are empowering children to become kinder and more responsible.

Psychologists, educators, and other experts agree. The National PTA Congress wrote:

> Children trained to extend justice, kindness, and mercy to animals become more just, kind, and considerate in their relations to each other. Character training along these lines will result in men and women of broader sympathies; more humane, more law abiding, in every respect more valuable citizens.

When children learn compassion and respect for animals, they are better able to extend compassion and respect to each other. A relationship with an animal also helps children gain self-confidence; research even indicates that being with an animal helps children relax and learn better. And by speaking out for those who cannot speak for themselves, children learn leadership and the power of their own voices to make the world a better place.

Village Earth Press has created this series of books because we believe that we need to take action on animals' behalf. We also believe that children should have opportunities to become all they can be. Our hope is that this book will contribute to both those goals.

Read more on this topic (and then discuss with children what you learn). We recommend these books:

The Emotional Lives of Animals
by Mark Bekoff

The Ten Trusts: What We Must Do to Care for the Animals We Love
by Jane Goodall

The Pig Who Sang to the Moon: The Emotional World of Farm Animals
by Jeffrey Moussaieff Masson

The Bond: Our Kinship with Animals, Our Call to Defend Them
by Wayne Pacelle

chapter 1
Dogs' Story

Have you ever heard the saying, "A dog is a man's best friend"? Really, cats and horses and other kinds of animals can also be a best friend to a human being. But it's true that dogs and humans have been together for a long, long time.

About 16,000 years ago, an animal that looked a lot like a gray wolf saw a campfire with human beings around it. He was curious, so he crept closer.

This animal was younger and smaller than the other males in his pack. That meant he often didn't have as much to eat as the bigger, stronger males did. He was afraid of the fire and people—but he was also VERY hungry. When he sniffed the air, he smelled good smells. The smell of food made him creep a little closer.

"Look," said a boy to his father. He pointed to the animal that was just outside the circle of firelight. "A wolf!"

His father reached for his spear, but then he stopped. He saw that the animal was small and thin. And something in his shiny dark eyes looked friendly. The man picked up a piece of meat from the fire. "Here you go, little brother," he said to the wolf. "We have enough to share."

The young wolf gulped down the meat in two bites.

The next night, he came back again to the campfire and the people. Each time, he came a little closer. Each time, the man and his son shared their meat with him. Finally, the young wolf became friends with the human beings. He played with the boy. He slept next to the man at night.

The humans soon learned that the animal was very smart. He was a good helper. He helped the humans follow the tracks of other animals they needed for food. And when a dangerous animal came near their homes in the night, the young wolf's loud barks woke up everyone—and scared away the dangerous animal. Even better, though, the wolf was so smart he almost seemed to understand what the humans were thinking. He soon learned to obey their commands. When they were sad, he leaned against them and licked their faces. He became their friend.

Dogs were the very first animals to be **domesticated**. They were the first animals to truly become friends with people. Other animals like goats and sheep, cows and chickens were domesticated because they gave food to people. But dogs were people's partners. They worked together.

What's that mean?

To be DOMESTICATED means that an animal has been tamed so that it can live with people.

Did You Know?

Scientists aren't sure where the first dogs started to live with humans, but they think it was in China or the Near East.

Did You Know?

All dogs—big and little, long-haired and short-haired—are descended from the gray wolf.

What's that mean?

An ARCHEOLOGIST is someone who digs up bones and other old things in order to learn more about the people who lived on the Earth a long time ago.

The AFTERLIFE is a way to talk about what happens when people and animals die. No one knows for sure what happens, but for thousands of years people have had lots of ideas about what happens after death.

Scientists study very old bones in order to understand how long dogs and people have been living together. They have found graves that are thousands of years old. Some of these graves have both people skeletons and dog skeletons. The way the dogs were buried shows that humans loved them. **Archeologists** have found graves like this all over the world—in Asia, Europe, Africa, and North America. Some dogs were buried just like people were. This means that the people who lived with these dogs thought of them as "people," not just as animals. They even left bowls of food for their dogs to snack on in the **afterlife**. Even thousands of years ago, people knew how much their dogs loved treats!

As people and dogs continued to live together, dogs became more and more important to people. Some people even believed dogs had magical powers. They also believed that their dogs loved them so much that they would stay with them even after death. In fact, people in many different places in the world, from India to the American Southwest, thought that dogs would lead them into the afterlife when they died. Death didn't seem as scary to them when their faithful dog would be waiting for them!

By a thousand years ago, most people no longer believed that dogs would show them the way to go when they died. But dogs were still important to people. Dogs helped people take care of sheep. They helped people hunt. They rescued people who were hurt, and they found people who were lost. They pulled sleds. They went to war with people and helped soldiers. They even became movie stars!

Dogs' Story

Famous Dogs

Munito was so smart that he convinced people he could add numbers and read the letters of the alphabet. He did tricks in a circus. ▶

Sergeant Stubby was in the American Army during World War I. He won medals for his bravery. ◀

Balto pulled a sled in Alaska that brought important medicine to sick people. ▼

In the 1930s, **Rin Tin Tin** was one of the first dogs to be an "actor." ▼

Rip helped rescue people from buildings that had been bombed in England in World War II. ▼

Not all brave dogs are big dogs. **Smoky** was a tiny Yorkshire terrier that stayed with her owner all though World War II while he was fighting in the jungles. She even had her own parachute that she used! ▶

Lassie had his own television show. ◀

Benji was a movie star dog. He starred in movies. ▶

Bo belongs to President Obama and his family. ◀

Dag helps soldiers in Iraq find bombs before they explode. ▶

Holly is a rescue dog who now helps wounded soldiers recover. ◀

Today people still love dogs. Some dogs are working dogs, but many more are just pets who share our homes. They keep us company. They make us feel better when we're sad. They play with us and make us laugh. More than a third of all American homes have at least one dog as a pet.

Dogs have come a long way since the wolf who crept up to that campfire. Dogs today come in all shapes and sizes. No other animal in the world can have so many different kinds of fur, different colors, and different sizes. There are more than 300 breeds of dogs!

Dogs' Story • 19

Ten Favorite Dog Breeds

Boxer

Boxers were once used for hunting. During wartime, they carried messages. Today, they are good pets because they love to please their families.

Yorkshire Terrier

Yorkies are tiny, but two hundred years ago in England, they had an important job — hunting rats. Today, they are bright and friendly little dogs who love their owners.

Golden Retriever

The golden retriever was first bred in Scotland for hunting. Today, golden retrievers are good pets for families with children because they are so gentle.

Beagle

These little dogs were used in England for hunting since the 1500s. Today, they're usually just pets.

Bulldog

Bulldogs are so ugly they're cute! They were once used in bull fights. Families like them as pets because they're so calm and good-natured.

Labrador Retriever

The Labrador retriever has been the most popular dog breed in the United States for more than twenty years, due to its gentle nature. Labs were once used by fishermen in Newfoundland to help round up fish and pull in nets. Later, they helped hunters.

Poodle

Poodles come from Germany, where hunters used them to bring back birds that fell into water. The "poodle clip" fur style was to protect the dogs' joints from cold water. Today, poodles come in three sizes, from tiny to large. They can be different colors.

German Shepherd

German shepherds were first bred in Germany in 1899. They've been used as guard dogs and by the police and the military—but they also make good family dogs. They are loyal and intelligent.

Dachshund

Dachshunds were used in Germany in the 1500s to dig out badgers from their underground dens. Today, their small size makes them a good choice for households where there won't be a lot of chances for them to get exercise.

Border Collie

Border collies are working dogs used for herding sheep in England and Scotland. They were specifically bred for intelligence and obedience. Their intelligence makes them wonderful family pets.

We love our dogs—but not all dogs have homes. Sometimes people think they want a dog, but then they decide their dog is too much work. They **abandon** their dogs. These dogs have to eat from garbage cans and catch wild animals for food. When these dogs have puppies, that means there will be even more homeless dogs.

Sometimes people think they only want a special kind of dog—like a poodle or a pug. They don't think they want a mutt. (A mutt is a dog that's a bunch of dog breeds all mixed together.) But mutts are just as intelligent and loving as any other

What's that mean?

ABANDON means to stop taking care of someone or something, to leave someone or something all alone.

Did You Know?

Scientists have found that having a dog helps people not get sick as much.

Did You Know?

The United States has more pet dogs than any other country in the world. Brazil is second in line, and China is third.

There are about 32 million pet dogs in the world. Another 20 million dogs are strays, who have no home.

dog. They need families to love them and take care of them.

And sometimes when people get the special kind of dog they thought they wanted, they find out the dog's not a good match for their family. Maybe she barks too much or she needs too much exercise. Teaching a dog to behave can be a lot of work! Some people don't want to go to all that work. When they abandon their pets, these dogs end up living in the streets. They too need someone to love them and care for them.

Animal shelters are places that take care of homeless animals. If your family has decided to get a dog—and that's a big decision—you can help out by getting your dog from a shelter instead of a pet store. You can do your part to help a dog who needs love.

Dogs' Story • 23

chapter 2
Finding Your New Best Friend

Do you love dogs? Do you wish you could have your very own puppy? Having a dog for your best friend is a wonderful thing. But there are things you should ask yourself before you get a dog.

First, are you **responsible**? Can people count on you to keep your promises? Do you always remember to do your chores? If you have a dog, he will depend on you. He will need you to take care of him even when you're tired or busy. You can't forget about your dog if you're having fun playing a game with your friends. If you're not willing to be responsible, you shouldn't get a dog. So be honest with yourself. When you get a dog, you are making a promise to him. You need to be able to keep your promise.

Next, ask yourself—do you know how to be gentle and kind to others? Or do you like to tease people? Are you ever mean? Dogs love to play. They may like to wrestle. But they also need people to be gentle with them. Their

> **What's that mean?**
>
> People who are RESPONSIBLE do their jobs even when they don't feel like it. They keep their promises. They do the things that others need them to do.

owners need to always be kind to them. Dogs count on their owners to never hurt them. It's never funny to tease or be mean to an animal.

Here's another question—do you have enough time to take care of a dog? Dogs need lots of attention. You can't just leave them alone in the backyard. They need to go for walks every day. They need exercise. They need people to spend time with them. If you do things after school every day, you might not have enough time to take good care of a dog. Make a list of all the things you have to do each day. How long are you at school? What do you do after school? How much homework do you have? How many chores do you have to do at home? After you've listed all these things, do you have time left over? Will you be able to spend enough time with a dog?

Once you've asked yourself these questions, do you feel like you're ready to have a dog? If you think you are, there are still more questions to ask before you get a dog or puppy.

Finding Your New Best Friend

What's that mean?

An **ALLERGY** makes people feel sick when they are around certain things. Some people are allergic to certain kinds of foods. They can get very sick if they eat those foods. A person who is allergic to dogs usually gets a runny nose when she's near a dog. She may sneeze a lot and have a hard time breathing. Her skin might get itchy.

If a dog has lots of **ENERGY**, he likes to run around a lot. It's hard for him to stay still. He doesn't get tired very easily.

A **VETERINARIAN**—or a vet—is a doctor for animals.

When a girl dog is **SPAYED**, she has an operation that makes it so she can't have puppies. A boy dog is **NEUTERED**, which means he gets an operation so he won't be able to make a girl dog have babies. These operations are important, because the world is already full of puppies that people don't want. You don't want your dog to make more puppies, unless you're sure you want them—and that those puppies will have good homes to go to when they grow up.

You don't live alone. There are other people who live in your home. Do they want a dog as much as you do? Is there anybody who is afraid of dogs? Or does anyone have an *allergy* to dogs? Do you have very young children in your family? Little kids don't always know to be gentle with dogs. If they're not gentle, they could hurt a dog, or the dog could hurt them. You also need to be sure that any other pets your family has will get along with your new dog. You don't want your new dog to hurt your other pets—and you don't want them to hurt your new dog. Before you decide to bring home a new friend, you want to make sure everyone will be safe!

If the others in your home are willing and able to have a dog join the family, is your home a good place for a dog? Do you have room for a dog? Different kinds of dogs need more room than others. If you get a small dog, she won't need as much space—but she will still need to go outside and go for walks. A big dog will need plenty of room to run around. Some dogs have lots of *energy*, other dogs are happier just lying around. If you live in a small apartment in a city, a smaller dog might be a better choice for you.

Does your family have enough money to take care of a dog? You will need to buy dog food. Keep in mind that a big dog will eat more than a little dog, so you will need to spend more money on food. Dogs also have to go to a *veterinarian*. They need shots every year to make sure they don't get sick. A girl dog should be *spayed*, and a boy dog needs to be *neutered*, and that costs money too.

Things you'll need before you bring home a dog:

Leash
Your dog needs a leash for going on walks.

Collar
Your dog's leash hooks on to his collar. Be sure you can always fit at least two fingers between the collar and your dog's skin. If you can't, the collar is too tight and you will need to buy a bigger one.

Tag
Your dog will need a tag on his collar. The tag should have your name, address, and phone number on it. That way if your dog gets lost, people can bring him home again.

Carrier Crate
If you need to take your dog to the vet or somewhere else, she should ride in a box like this where she'll be safe.

Finding Your New Best Friend

Dog Food

Dogs eat dry food, but they can also have food that comes in a can.

Food and Water Dishes

Dogs need both food and water every day. The water bowl should always have water in it, so they can get a drink whenever they want.

Dog Bed

Your dog will need somewhere to sleep. A bed like this is especially made for a dog, but he could be just as happy with an old blanket in a box. What's important is that he has a place to sleep that belongs just to him.

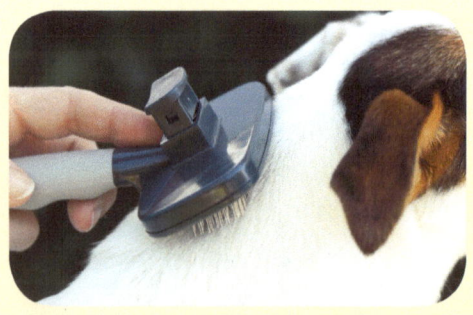

Brush

Pet stores sell special brushes that are made just for dogs. If you brush your dog often, she won't shed so much hair. If she has long hair, brushing will keep her from getting snarls and mats in her fur.

Toys

Dogs like to play. They'll play fetch with a stick, but they love to chase balls even more. Toys can keep dogs from getting bored when they have to be alone. They'll get into less mischief if they have toys to play with.

Chew Bones

Dogs need to chew on things—and you probably won't want them to chew on your shoes or your schoolbooks! Chew bones also help keep dogs' teeth clean.

Shampoo

Your dog needs to take baths, just like you do. Dogs who play outside can get muddy. Dogs can also start to smell bad if they don't get baths often enough. Pet stores sell shampoo that's made especially for dogs. You could also use baby shampoo, which is gentle enough for dogs' skin and won't hurt their eyes.

Here are things your dog may not need—
but they may be helpful to have, depending
on what your dog is like.

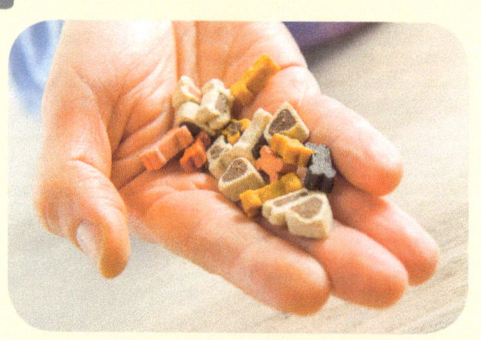

Treats

Dogs love special treats. They shouldn't have too many—any more than you should eat too many snacks—but you can get healthy dog treats at a pet store. You can also use treats to help you train your dog.

Clippers

Cutting your dog's claws will keep them from getting too long and sharp. It's not an easy job, though, so you should ask a grown-up to do it—or you might want to have your vet or a groomer do the job for you. It needs to be done right, so that your dog doesn't bleed.

Sweaters

If your dog is small or short-haired, she may need to wear a sweater to keep her warm when she goes outside, especially if you live somewhere that the winters are very cold.

Baby Gate

If you don't want your dog to go in certain parts of your house, a baby gate is a good way to keep him out. You might want to use one just when you're away from home, to make sure he stays in areas where he's safe and won't get into trouble.

Potty Pads

If you have a puppy that is learning where she should go to the bathroom and where she shouldn't, pads can help her not make messes on the floor. They soak up the pee and make it easy to clean up.

Spray Cleaner

All dogs make messes once in a while, and puppies usually make lots of messes before they learn not to pee and poop on the floor. Pet stores sell cleaner that's made especially to clean up animal messes.

Dog House

If your dog is going to spend time outside, he needs to have a shelter. You should never leave a dog outside without a place where he can go to get out of the hot sun, the cold, and the rain.

Harness

Some dogs pull on their leashes when they go for a walk. They can pull so hard they hurt their throats. A harness can be a good way to keep this from happening. It can also make it easier to control a dog than just a collar. A dog can't slip her head out of a harness the way she might with a collar.

What's that mean?

A PUREBRED dog comes from parents who looked like him—and their parents (and THEIR parents) looked the same as well. They were all the same breed. Collies, German shepherds, poodles, and Labradors are all breeds. A **MIXED-BREED** dog is sometimes called a "mutt." Her parents were not the same breed. Her mother and father may have been two different kinds of purebreds, or they might have been a mixture of breeds too.

If you're sure you are ready to bring a dog into your family, there are MORE things to think about. What kind of dog do you want—big or small, mixed-breed or purebred, puppy or adult dog? Will a small dog fit best into your family? Do you have time to train a puppy?

If you get a purebred puppy, you will know certain things about her that you

Rottweilers are big dogs, but they are usually gentle and loving. When they're happy they sometimes make a noise that sounds a little like growling—but it's actually more like a cat's purr. They like to lean against people. This is something they learned to do back in the days when people used them to work with cows. They would lean their weight against a cow to make it go in the direction it was supposed to go.

CARING FOR DOGS

might not know about a mixed-breed puppy. You'll know how big or little she will be once she grows up. You will know if she will shed a lot of hair or hardly any at all. Some breeds—like terriers and border collies—have lots of energy, so if you get one of these puppies, expect them to need lots of exercise. Other breeds—like bulldogs and basset hounds—don't need to move around as much. Some breeds are usually good with children, like Labradors and golden retrievers.

But you can't be CERTAIN what a dog will be like, even if she belongs to a breed. Every dog is different. And there are also good reasons for getting a mixed-breed dog. Mixed-breeds are just as smart and loving as purebreds. Many times, they're also healthier than

Puppy or Full-Grown Dog?

Everyone loves puppies. They're SO cute! But they're also a lot of work. They can chew on things and sometimes ruin them. Puppies have accidents on the floor, because they don't know yet where they're supposed to pee and poop. Like human babies, they need a lot of attention. They need to be taught all the things they need to learn—like where to go to the bathroom, how to behave in new places, how to get along with other animals, and where they're allowed to go and where they're not allowed. It's hard work to teach them all those things. An adult dog, however, may already know all those things. She might be a better choice if your family doesn't have a lot of time to train a puppy.

Did You Know?

People don't adopt black puppies and dogs as often as they do other colors—so there are lots of black puppies like this one who need good homes.

Every Dog's Dream rescues dogs that have no homes—and then matches them up with families who can take care of them.

purebreds. They might live longer and get sick less.

You need to think about all these things BEFORE you go to pick out your dog or puppy. Otherwise, it's too easy to fall in love with the cutest face. Remember—the puppy who looks the cutest might not really be the best match for your family. So it's a good idea to make up your mind ahead of time about what you and your family want.

It's also easy to walk through a pet store and decide you want one of the puppies there. But many purebred puppies come from "puppy mills." These are places that keep mother dogs just to get lots of puppies to sell. The mother dogs often have bad lives. Their puppies may be cute, but they may also have lots of problems you can't see at first. They may have health problems. They may have **temperament** problems.

The best place to find your new best friend is at a shelter or dog rescue. These are dogs that need homes. You can find purebreds and mixed-breed dogs at a shelter, puppies and older dogs, big dogs and little dogs. The people who work at the shelter can help match you with the best dog for you. When you take him home, you'll know you're doing a good thing. That dog needs YOU!

What's that mean?

TEMPERAMENT is what a person or animal is like most of the time. Some people, for example, have calm temperaments, while others have nervous temperaments. This doesn't mean that a person with a calm temperament never feels nervous—or a person with a nervous temperament never feels calm. A person's temperament is how she is most of the time. Animals, including dogs, have temperaments too, the same way people do. A dog might have a gentle temperament, or he might be the sort of dog that gets into fights easily.

chapter 3
Keeping Your Dog Healthy

When you feel sick, you can say, "I have a stomachache." Or you might say, "My head hurts," or, "My throat is sore." You can let the grown-ups in your family know that you're not feeling well. If you need to go to the doctor, you can tell her more about how you feel. The doctor will listen to you, and she will use what you say to help her understand why you are sick.

But your dog can't tell you when he's feeling sick! He can't say that he has a sore paw, and he can't tell you if his stomach is upset. He's counting on you to keep him healthy—but he can't tell you what he needs. You'll need to learn what to do to keep him from getting sick.

There are quite a few things your dog needs. If you do these things, you'll help keep him healthy.

Make sure your dog has fresh water all the time.

Like all living creatures, dogs need water. Your dog should always have water in her bowl. Whenever the water gets a little low, fill up the bowl again. Once a day, dump out the old water, rinse out the bowl, and put in fresh, clean water. Keep your dog's water bowl somewhere she can get to it whenever she wants—and where no one will bump it and tip it over.

Feed your dog healthy food.

Eating the right foods is one of the things that keeps you healthy—and it will help keep your dog healthy too. Good food will make your dog's fur shiny and thick. It will help him not get sick. It could even make him live longer.

Most adult dogs only need to eat once a day. They don't need breakfast, lunch, and dinner the way you do. Never forget to feed your dog! But also be careful not to feed your dog too much. It's okay to give your dog treats sometimes between meals—just don't give her too many. Some dogs will overeat, like some people do. When a dog eats too much, she will get fat, and being fat isn't good for dogs. It could make them get sick or not live as long.

On hot days, dogs need to drink more water, just like you do. But dogs can't sweat the way you do. Instead, they stick out their tongues and pant. Panting helps dogs cool off the way sweating helps people cool off.

Most dogs love people food. Some people food is good for them, but some isn't. Never give your dog these foods:

- chocolate
- grapes or raisins
- onions
- bones (because they can splinter and get caught in your dog's throat)

These people foods are good for dogs (so long as they don't eat too much and get fat):

- peanut butter
- cooked chicken
- yoghurt
- cheese
- eggs
- green beans
- pumpkin
- carrots
- apple slices

Take your dog to the vet at least once a year.

Your dog needs to go to a veterinarian for checkups, the same way you need to go to the doctor. The vet will give your dog the shots he needs, to keep him from getting sick. She will check his teeth, his heart, and his ears. She will be able to tell you what kind of food is best for your dog and how much.

Your vet will also keep your dog from getting **parasites**—or get rid of them if your dog already has them. Dogs can get fleas, ticks, heartworms, and **intestinal** worms. Fleas are tiny bugs that will make your dog very itchy. They will also make YOU very itchy if they jump off your dog and bite you. Ticks are another kind of small insect that bite dogs. Ticks carry diseases, so a tick bite could make your dog very sick. Worms can live in your dog's heart and intestines. Heartworms can kill dogs, but you don't have to let that happen. Your vet will have ways to protect your dog from all kinds of parasites.

When you first get a dog, you should take her to see a vet right away. The vet will check to see if your dog has fleas or worms. He will give her any shots she needs. If you have a puppy, she may need to come back for more shots after a few months. Once she is an adult dog, she only needs to go to the vet once a year. Of course, if your dog hurts herself or gets sick, you

What's that mean?

PARASITES are living things that live off another living thing. Parasites that live on or in your dog get their food from your dog's body.

INTESTINAL is a word people use for talking about intestines, the long tubes inside your body where food is digested.

should call your vet right away. He will tell you if your dog needs to come into his office to get medicine.

If you get a puppy or dog that hasn't been spayed or neutered, it's important that you have your vet do that too. When a girl dog is spayed, she can no longer have puppies. When a boy dog is neutered, he can no longer make a girl dog pregnant. There are already too many puppies and dogs in the world that don't have homes. You don't want your dog to add to the problem.

Spaying and neutering are operations. The vet will put your dog to sleep first. Then he will make a cut in your dog's body and take out the parts that make babies. Once the vet is done, he will sew up the cut. When your dog wakes up, she will feel sore. She won't be able to play for a few days. She will need you to be extra nice to her.

Give your dog a place to sleep.

If your dog spends part of his time outside, he will need a dog house where he can go to get out of the sun, rain, wind, and cold. The house should be in the shade, so that it doesn't get too hot in the summer. It should be big enough for your dog to turn around inside it.

Puppies need to eat more often than grown-up dogs do, and they need a different kind of dog food from what adult dogs eat. Old dogs may also need to eat differently from younger dogs.

Did You Know?

One female flea lays up to 2,000 eggs. That means if your dog had just one flea, she could soon have LOTS of fleas.

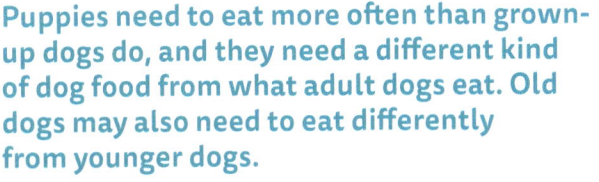

Dogs need you to take care of their teeth. Your vet can tell you the best way to do this. Some people even brush their dogs' teeth!

Put an old blanket or straw on the bottom of the house for bedding. When the bedding gets dirty, either wash the blanket or throw out the old straw and put in fresh straw.

When your dog is inside your house, she needs a bed that's all her own. Some people have their dogs sleep in a crate. Dogs like crates because they seem like cozy little dens. The bottom of the crate should always have something soft on it. You can also buy dog beds at a pet store. Dogs like to know they have their own places that belong just to them.

Make sure your dog gets plenty of exercise.

People need to exercise to be healthy, and so do dogs. Getting enough exercise will help your dog not get fat. Dogs also need exercise to keep them from getting in trouble. If you take your dog for a long walk every day, he'll be less likely to do things you don't want him to (like bark a lot or chew on things he shouldn't). Make sure he has plenty of water to drink after exercising.

Play with your dog.

Playing is another way to make sure your dog gets the exercise she needs, but it also keeps your dog from getting bored. Dogs love to play! They like to play fetch with balls and sticks and Frisbees. They also like toys that squeak. Most of all, dogs like doing things with the people they love. When you have fun with your friends, it helps you feel close to them—and when you and your dog have fun together, it will help you become good friends.

Give your dog things to chew on.

Dogs love to chew on things, and puppies love to chew even more than grown-up dogs do. Sometimes dogs chew on things you don't want them to chew on—like your shoes, your schoolbooks, or your toys. If you give them chew toys and chew treats, they will be less likely to chew on things they're not supposed to.

Chewing also helps keep your dog's teeth clean. Some chew treats are like toothbrushes for dogs. Your vet will be able to tell you what chew treats are healthiest for your dog.

Take care of your dog's fur.

Some dogs have long hair, and some have short. Some shed a lot of fur, and some shed just a little. Long hair or short, fluffy or silky, all dogs need to be brushed.

If you have a long-haired dog, you may need to brush her once a day.

Did You Know?
Dog groomers give dogs baths, cut their hair, brush them, and trim their claws. A dog groomer is like a beauty salon for dogs!

Dogs can't understand everything people say—but they CAN learn what some words mean. Dogs learn words like "walk," "sit," "ride," and "bed," but they can also learn other words. Scientists say that most dogs can understand more than 100 words!

Some kinds of dogs get snarls in their fur if they're not brushed often. Brushing also keeps your dog from shedding so much fur on furniture and carpets. Short-haired dogs don't need to be brushed as often.

Some dogs need haircuts. If you have a long-haired dog, he might be more comfortable in the summer if you cut off some of his fur. Other dogs have fur that keeps on growing all the time, the way the hair on your head does. If these dogs don't get haircuts, their fur becomes too long. Don't try to cut your dog's hair yourself! A grown-up should do it, or you can take your dog to a dog groomer.

Dogs need baths too. For one thing, dogs love to get dirty. They get muddy playing outside. They like to roll in stinky things. Dogs also need a bath about once a month, even if they haven't done anything to get dirty. If they don't have baths, they get smelly.

Where your dog gets her bath will depend on how big she is. If she's little, you can give her a bath in the kitchen sink. If she's too big to fit in the sink, she can get her bath in the same bathtub you use. If it's not cold, you could also give her a bath outside.

When you wash your dog, make sure the water isn't too hot or too cold. Use baby shampoo or special dog shampoo. Try not to get soap in his eyes or let water go in his ears. Don't push your fingers or a sponge inside his ears, but you should wash the outside parts of his ears.

When you're done, rinse out all the soap. If you don't, your dog's skin could get dry and itchy. Once he's well rinsed, use a towel to get him as dry as you can.

Some dogs like their baths. Some dogs hate them. If your dog doesn't like bath time, don't yell at her. That will make her hate her bath even more. Talk to her gently. Tell her what a good dog she is when she holds still. Give her a treat when she's all done. If she learns she gets a treat every time she has a bath, she won't mind being washed so much.

Give your dog lots of attention.

Dogs love attention. Your dog may not understand what you say when you talk to him, but he likes to hear your voice. He likes to be near to you. He needs to know you love him—and he wants to show you that he loves you too! A grown-up dog will be okay being home alone while you're at school, but don't leave him alone for much longer than that. Dogs get lonely, just like people do.

Just like people need love, so do dogs. In fact, more than anything else, your dog needs your love. If you love your dog, you will do everything you can to take good care of her. It's your job to look after her, the same way the grown-ups in your life look after you. She is counting on you take good care of her.

Your dog needs YOU!

Most dogs love to go for a ride. Never leave your dog alone in the car for very long, though. If you have to leave him for a few minutes, make sure the car is parked in the shade. Roll down the windows a little—but not so far that he can jump out. If it's hot, don't leave your dog in the car at all. Dogs left in hot cars can die.

chapter 4
Understanding Your Dog

If you get a dog, you'll find out you have a lot in common. Your dog will like things that make him feel happy. He'll like to play. He will feel sad when someone yells at him. Sometimes he might feel angry if someone tries to take something that is his. He'll feel lonely when he's by himself too long. He'll get bored when there's nothing to do.

But in some ways a dog and you are very different from each other. For one thing, you speak different languages! He can't tell you with words how he's feeling. He'll tell you in other ways, though. Mostly, he'll use his body. That's called body language. You'll have to learn to understand him.

Here are some of the ways you can tell what your dog is feeling:

When your dog rolls on her back, belly up, that means she's happy, she loves you, and she trusts you.

If your dog stands with his head up, his ears up, and his tail up, the way this dog is doing, that means he's alert. He's interested in something, and he's paying close attention to it. This is how you want him to look when you're teaching him something.

When your dog lies like this, she may be feeling a little bored. She's just hanging out, waiting for something interesting to happen.

Understanding Your Dog

A dog who is feeling sad will put his head down. His ears will go down too. Bored and sad can look a lot alike for a dog.

When a dog puts her head, tail, and ears down, she's feeling scared. She might also look like this when you yell at her for doing something she shouldn't. Then it means, "I'm sorry. Please forgive me!"

A dog who puts his butt up and his front down is asking you to play with him.

When your dog tips her head to one side like this dog is doing, she's asking you a question. She might be saying, "Are you coming?" Or she might be asking, "Did I just hear you say we're going for a WALK?"

This dog is telling his owner, "I love you. I'm ready to do whatever you want. Let's go have some fun."

These two dogs have just met each other. The brown dog is asking the black dog to play—but the black dog is feeling a little scared. You can tell because his legs are stiff, and his tail is held very high.

This dog is angry. Her ears are back, and her lips are pulled back too, so that you can see her teeth. If you see a dog looking like this, stay away. She's saying, "I might bite you!"

This dog is saying, "What you're doing feels really good. I love you. I'm so happy to be with you."

Understanding Your Dog

Dogs may not be able to say words, but they learn to understand some of the words people use. Their favorite words are often "walk" and "ball"!

Dogs also use their voices to **communicate**. They have different ways of barking when they want to say different things. One bark by itself might mean, "I want to come inside." It could mean, "Come on, I'm waiting for you." If your dog barks a lot, very loudly, he might be saying, "Someone I don't know is outside your house! Be careful!" Sometimes, a dog can bark and bark just because he's bored. When a dog whines, he might be sad. He might be bored and hoping you'll do something—like throw a ball for him or give him a treat. He might also be feeling sick or in pain. Dogs can growl for different reasons too. Their growls may mean,

What's that mean?

When you COMMUNICATE with someone, you tell them something. You give them a message. There are all sorts of ways that people communicate. They talk, they send letters, they talk on the phone, they e-mail, they text, and they post on Facebook. People also use body language to communicate, the same as dogs do. A smile, a shrug, a bowed head, and folded arms are all forms of human body language.

It's okay to scold your dog when she does something she's not supposed to do. But make sure she understands why you're scolding her. Say when you get to school, you find out your dog stole your lunch out of your backpack. If you scold her when you get home from school, she's not going to know why you're angry with her. She'll just feel confused and sad. And no matter what your dog does, it's NEVER okay to hit her, kick her, or hurt her in any way.

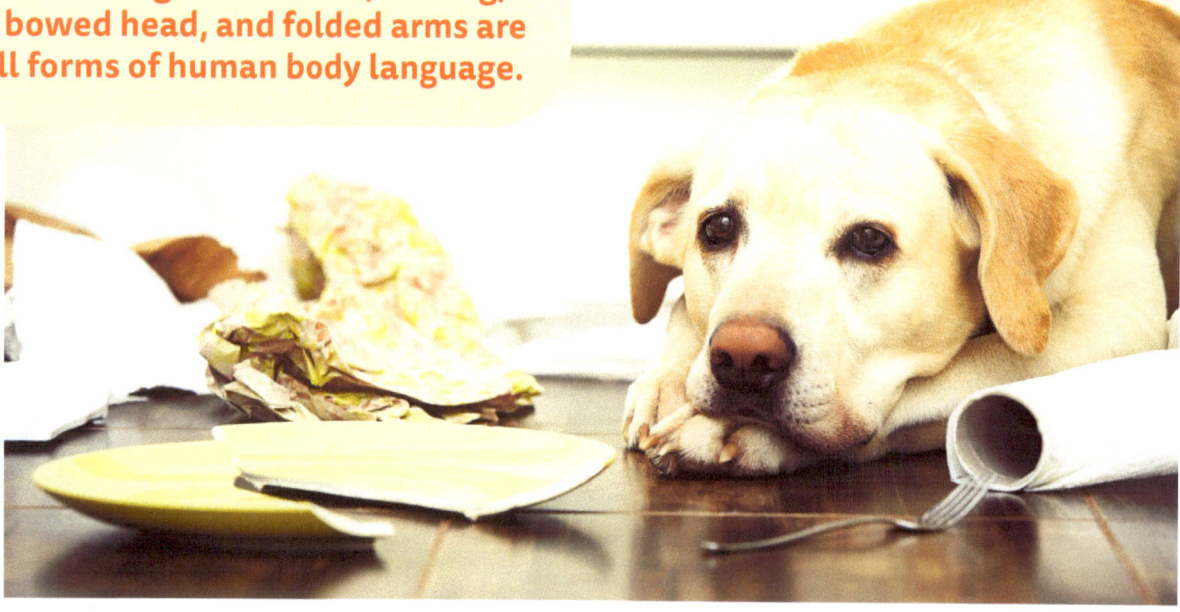

There are many pit bulls that have no homes—but many people won't adopt a pit bull. They think pit bulls are dangerous and scary. They think that all pit bulls bite! That's not true, though. Scientists have studied pit bulls. They found that pit bulls don't bite any more than other dogs. In fact, pit bulls are actually one of the most good-natured dogs there are. Any dog that's been treated cruelly can learn to bite to protect herself, and you should always be careful with any dog you don't know. But there's no need to be afraid of pit bulls more than other dogs!

"Keep away from me!" When they growl with their lips pulled back from their teeth, they may be saying, "Watch out! I might bite you!" But dogs also growl when they're playing. Those aren't mean growls. They're just a way dogs like to play make-believe. The longer you know your dog, the more you'll be able to understand her barks, whines, and growls. Understanding your dog will help you be a better friend to her.

You should never, ever be mean to your dog or hurt her in anyway.

But it IS your job to be in charge—not the other way around. Your dog needs to know you are the boss. She needs to listen when you tell her to do something. She shouldn't think that she's the one in charge.

Your dog will need you to teach him lots of things. It will be your job to teach him how to behave around people he doesn't know. You will teach him where he can poop and pee—and where he can't. You'll teach him where he's allowed to go, and where he isn't.

A wolf lives in a group of other wolves called a pack. The pack always has a leader, and the other wolves obey the leader. Your dog will think of your family as his pack. He needs to know you are the leader. That way he will do what you tell him to.

Did You Know?

Wolves and dogs have the same body language. If you can understand what your dog is saying with his body, you'll be able to understand wolf body language too!

You'll also teach him to obey commands like "sit," "stay," and "come." You might want to teach him tricks, like "shake," "high five," and "roll over."

Dogs like to learn new things. It keeps them from getting bored. The more time you spend with your dog, teaching her things, the happier she will be.

When dogs are bored, they often get in trouble. They may bark too much. They might chew on things they're not supposed to. They often get too excited when they see new people, barking and jumping and running around in circles. Spending time every day teaching your dog new things will help her be a calmer, better-behaved dog.

If your dog gets plenty of exercise, that will also help him stay out of trouble. All dogs need to exercise, and some dogs need more than other dogs do. The more exercise he gets, the better behaved he will be.

All dogs get in trouble sometimes, just like kids do. Most times, when your dog does something wrong,

A good way to teach your dog to obey commands is to take her to an obedience class. That way she'll learn how to behave—and at the same time, you'll be learning how to teach her.

Understanding Your Dog • 51

When you teach your dog to sit, you can use both your hands and your voice to communicate with her. Be sure to praise her when she does what you asked her to do. At first, you might also give your dog a little treat each time she obeys you.

there's a reason. Maybe she's bored. Maybe she's not getting enough exercise. Maybe she isn't getting enough chances to go outside. Don't just yell at her. Pay attention to what she's trying to tell you. See if there is something you can do to help her behave better.

It feels good when someone understands you. The people who understand you best are the people you like being with. They're your friends and your family. They're the people you love, the people who love you. You have fun together. And it works the same way with your dog. The more you understand him, the better you can get along. He'll know you love him—and he'll love you back.

Don't forget—your dog is counting on you. She needs you to understand her!

Here are some books and websites that will help you and your family understand and teach your dog:

Good Dog; Bad Dog (A 10 Step Dog Training Program)
by Ivan King

Good Dog! Kids Teach Kids About Dog Behavior and Training
by Evelyn Pang

How to Speak Dog: A Guide to Decoding Dog Language
by Aline Alexandra Newman and Gary Weitzman

How to Love Your Dog: A Kid's Guide to Dog Care
www.loveyourdog.com

Dog Training: 5 Tricks Kids Can Teach the Dog
www.kidspot.com.au/kids-activities-and-games/Outdoor-activities+9/Dog-training-5-tricks-kids-can-teach-the-dog+12102.htm

Understanding Your Dog

Image Credits

Cover: Micaela Grace Sanna, Nivi (Dreamstime), Sickyicky (Dreamstime), Ustel65 (Dreamstime)

Pages 1–4: Andrey Puhash (Dreamstime), Anke Van Wyk (Dreamstime), Chantal Ringuette (Dreamstime), Daniela Jakob (Dreamstime), Eckwahl-Sanna, Ksenia Raykova (Dreamstime), Mariaphotography10 (Dreamstime), Micaela Grace Sanna, Nivi (Dreamstime), Pixbilder (Dreamstime), Roughcollie (Dreamstime), Sunheyy (Dreamstime), Sunheyy (Dreamstime), Voyagerix (Dreamstime)

Introduction: Lenka Šošolíková (Dreamstime), Micaela Grace Sanna

Chapter 1: Breannarae (Dreamstime), Cristina Annibali (Dreamstime), Dragoneye (Dreamstime), cynoclub (Shutterstock), Eduard Kyslynskyy (Dreamstime), Eric Isselee (Shutterstock), Ksenia Raykova (Dreamstime), Micaela Grace Sanna, Michelle De Kock (Dreamstime), Muro123 (Dreamstime), otsphoto (Shutterstock), Pavla Zakova (Dreamstime), Przemyslaw Zamirski (Dreamstime), Pumba1 (Dreamstime), randomela (Dreamstime), Tomislav Birtic (Dreamstime), Utekhina Anna (Shutterstock), Volodymyr Finoshkin (Dreamstime), Yogiproductions (Dreamstime), Yokeetod (Dreamstime)

Chapter 2: Antonio Gravante (Dreamstime), Bucur Petre (Dreamstime), Christine Bird (Dreamstime), Damedeeso (Dreamstime), Dana Kenneth Johnson (Dreamstime), Denys Kuvaiev (Dreamstime), Eduardo Gonzalez Diaz (Dreamstime), Eric Isselee (Shutterstock), Gvictoria (Dreamstime), Ingemar Magnusson (Dreamstime), Jackbluee (Dreamstime), Jennie Magro (Dreamstime), Joruba (Dreamstime), Karenr (Dreamstime), Katarzyna Bialasiewicz (Dreamstime), Lilofantastico (Dreamstime), Mexitographer (Dreamstime), Micaela Grace Sanna, Monika Wisniewska (Dreamstime), Padufoto (Dreamstime), Rory Trappe (Dreamstime), Simone Winkler (Dreamstime), Tab1962 (Dreamstime), Tiverylucky (Dreamstime)

Chapter 3: Atiger88 (Dreamstime), Diana Eller (Dreamstime), Jaroslav Frank (Dreamstime), Mexitographer (Dreamstime), Micaela Grace Sanna, Piotr Rydzkowski (Dreamstime), Willeecole (Dreamstime)

Chapter 4: Anna Yakimova (Dreamstime), Brett Critchley (Dreamstime), Carolannefreeling (Dreamstime), Crystal Craig (Dreamstime), Eric Isselee (Shutterstock), Goldenkb (Dreamstime), Ian Allenden (Dreamstime), James Boardman (Dreamstime), Jaromír Chalabala (Dreamstime), Jojjik (Dreamstime), Lifeontheside (Dreamstime), Marcelo Vildósola Garrigó (Dreamstime), Micaela Grace Sanna, Nikolay Pozdeev (Dreamstime), Pojoslaw (Dreamstime), Rodrusoleg (Dreamstime), Templario2004 (Dreamstime), Walter Arce (Dreamstime), Yuriy Zelenen'kyy (Dreamstime)

Pages 55-58: Anke Van Wyk (Dreamstime), Dmitri Maruta (Dreamstime), Duccio (Dreamstime), Fotooxotnik (Dreamstime), Irina Tiumentseva (Dreamstime), Jaroslav Noska (Dreamstime), Micaela Grace Sanna, Pavla Zakova (Dreamstime), Photowitch (Dreamstime), Pixbilder (Dreamstime), Puttipong Thephussadin N Ayutaya (Dreamstime), Qliebin (Dreamstime), Reddogs (Dreamstime), Reddogs (Dreamstime), Roughcollie (Dreamstime), Sergey Uryadnikov (Dreamstime), Sickyicky (Dreamstime), Sigurdur William Brynjarsson (Dreamstime), Sommai Sommai (Dreamstime), Sunheyy (Dreamstime), Ustel65 (Dreamstime), Vitaliy Hrabar (Dreamstime), Zanna Peshnina (Dreamstime)

www.ingramcontent.com/pod-product-compliance
Lightning Source LLC
Chambersburg PA
CBHW061358090426
42743CB00002B/60